Open Hearts

By Jane Seymour

RUNNING PRESS

PHILADELPHIA · LONDON

9 8 7 6 5 4 3
Digit on the right indicates the number of this printing

Library of Congress Control Number: 2008932641

ISBN 978-0-7624-3662-0

Designed by Maria Taffera Lewis
Edited by Cindy De La Hoz
Typography: Futura, Granjon, and P22 Cezanne

Running Press Book Publishers
2300 Chestnut Street
Philadelphia, PA 19103-4371

Visit us on the web!
www.runningpress.com

Dedications

♡

From Jane:
To my husband James, our children,
my sisters Sally and Anne,
and especially to my mother Mieke,
whose heart overflowed with love

From Sally:
To my mother, Ceris

Peace, Love, and an Open Heart

Contents

An Open Heart

IN MY LIFE, I HAVE HAD MY HEART BROKEN MANY TIMES. We all have. I'm not just thinking of the love affair that goes wrong, the marriage that falls apart; I'm thinking of the pain when a child suffers, when work goes wrong, when you lose someone you care for. We have all nursed broken hearts.

While painting one morning, I found I was drawing simple sketches of hearts over and over, with a kind of sadness. It was as though the conventional heart shape seemed almost too closed. It suggested neat, loving people, each cut off from the other, each enclosed as if to protect themselves from pain. And I relaxed and began to sketch more openly, more fluidly, and the hearts were slightly open, more hopeful, like a door being opened.

As I drew, I found the hearts linking together, and I experienced an extraordinary mix of peace and excitement which hasn't left me. It came to me that we are all linked under the same skies, every one of us. We are all experiencing the same glorious opera of life. Open and linked, receptive and loving; the linked hearts are not broken, but open. But the linked heart is not just about loving and giving; it is about being receptive to your own voice, to your own talents, and to your opportunities. The open heart doesn't say, "No, I can't do that." It says, "Yes, I'm open to change, open to challenges. This is my one shot at life!"

An open heart doesn't make you vulnerable to intruders; it makes you invulnerable, because you know you can survive. You can let go of what is upsetting, really hurtful, really tough, and allow something beautiful and new to enter. If your heart is open, it can never stay broken.

I wanted to compile a book which celebrated and explored the idea of the open heart, which was not merely heartwarming but heart opening. Keep this book by your bed. Consult it when the going gets tough. Send it to a friend who is going through a bad time. This book celebrates life and will help you to live it more richly and rewardingly. It mixes the thoughts of inspirational writers with those of ordinary people. It explores the tolerance that is the basis of real and enduring happiness.

Above all, this book will show you how to be tolerant of yourself. My mother would tell me, "You can't truly love someone else until you love yourself," and I know she was right. She died recently, and this book is in part for her, because she had such an open heart. She gave and gave, and you know, the more she gave of her hospitality, her time, and her advice, the more she received. My sisters and I often encounter our mother's friends in our travels. They say, "Oh, Mieke, we used to stay with her; we loved her so," and they look after us as our mother once looked after them. For the open heart is not stopped by death; the open heart continues.

After my divorce I felt I could never trust or love again. I had too much pain and baggage ever to be free to love and be loved. Then I met James. He astounded me with his ability to see through the happy exterior I could simulate so well, performer that I am, and he asked me what or who could have made me so full of pain. His open-hearted gesture to dare ask, and then truly to listen, allowed me to let go of all the hurt and judgments I harbored about myself and others. He loved me "warts and all" and continues to fifteen years later.

If James hadn't helped me to open my heart again, we would not have known the amazing life we now have—six kids, varied careers, life adventures, and so much love from friends and family. I dared to be vulnerable and to trust and it has shown me that to live with an open heart is the only way to experience life to the fullest.

Of course, the open heart is about love. I am not talking just about romantic love, but love for yourself, love for your talents, and love for the exquisite beauty of the natural world. It is love for your neighbors, your friends, your family, and love of God, in whatever form you happen to find Him. For the open heart is, more than anything else, about tolerance, about seeing beyond the petty into the greater picture. It is the opposite of hate. In this present world of division and intolerance, we need open hearts.

—JANE SEYMOUR

Connect

The Secret of Happiness

♡

HOW TO BE AT PEACE NOW? By making peace with the present moment. The present moment is the field on which the game of life happens. It cannot happen anywhere else. Once you have made peace with the present moment, see what happens, what you can do or choose to do, or rather, what life does through you. There are three words that convey the secret of the art of living, the secret of all success and happiness: One With Life. Being one with life is being one with Now. You then realize that you don't live your life, but life lives you. Life is the dancer, and you are the dance.

—ECKHART TOLLE

Here's to Today

♡

Look to this day! For it is life, the very life of life.

For yesterday is but a dream.

And tomorrow is only a vision. But today well lived makes

every yesterday a dream of happiness.

And tomorrow a vision of hope.

Look well, therefore, to this day!

—*Sanskrit Proverb*

We Are One

♡

There is no greatest nation.

There is no true religion.

There is no inherently perfect philosophy.

There is no always right political party,

morally supreme economic system,

or one and only way to heaven.

Erase these ideas from your memory.

Eliminate them from your experience.

Eradicate them from your culture.

For these are thoughts of division and separation,

and you have killed each other over these thoughts.

Only the truth I give you here will save you:

We Are One.

Carry this message far and wide, across oceans

and over continents, around the corner

and around the world.

—*Neale Donald Walsch*

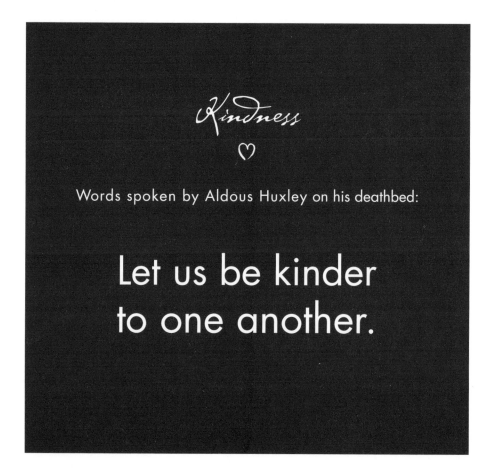

Kindness

♡

Words spoken by Aldous Huxley on his deathbed:

Let us be kinder to one another.

How Did He Live?

♡

Not how did he die, but how did he live?

Not what did he gain, but what did he give?

These are the units to measure the worth

of a man as a man, regardless of birth.

Not what was his church, nor what was his creed?

But had he befriended those really in need?

Was he ever ready, with word of good cheer,

To bring back a smile, to banish a tear?

Not what did the sketch in the newspaper say,

But how many were sorry when he passed away.

—ANONYMOUS

When All Is Said and Done

♡

LIKE HIS FATHER BEFORE HIM, my husband, James Keach, has devoted himself to films and television as a director, producer, and actor. Caught up in the most glamorous business in the world, it can be easy to lose sight of "the greater picture."

Filmmakers spend much of their lives worrying about how high the grosses and ratings of their movies and television shows will be. Yes, this matters, but when we leave behind our contribution to history, I do not think this is why our time on earth will have mattered.

When, perchance, we come face to face with our maker, I do not believe He will ask us what the grosses of our movies were or what our bank balance was. I believe we will be asked what we did for our brothers and sisters, mothers and fathers, our children, and the people we may not know by name.

What positive difference did I make in their lives? How much love did I leave behind? Did I live with an open heart?

—JAMES KEACH

Love is Strong

♡

WHEN MY FORMER CO-STAR and dear friend Christopher Reeve had his horseback-riding accident, he and his wife, Dana, showed the world how to open your heart when life seems insurmountable. Chris gave all his energy to advance knowledge globally about spinal cord injuries and other diseases. Dana showed the love and courage of a caregiver. They inspire me daily and will always be remembered for their courage and love.

Place me like a seal over your heart,

like a seal on your arm;

For love is as strong as death,

its jealousy unyielding as the grave.

It burns like blazing fire,

like a mighty flame.

Many waters cannot quench love;

rivers cannot wash it away.

If one were to give all the wealth of his house for love,

it would be utterly scorned.

—*SONG OF SONGS (8: 6-7)*

First Love, First Heartbreak

♡

I'VE NEVER FORGOTTEN the feeling of complete elation that comes with first love.

It was a scary, foreign feeling, yet light as the flight of a butterfly. The moment I tried to hang on to it, it changed, and when he ultimately moved on to another girl, my heart was broken. I turned to my mother and cried inconsolably, gasping for breath, and feeling that my life was over. She listened and showed no judgment—just an open heart.

Though I had lost that first love, in time this led me to the amazing discovery that I belonged to a world filled with people who had experienced the same pain and could learn to love again. Similarly, my bond with my mother was reborn that day she helped me through my first heartbreak. I continue to ask her advice. Even though she has passed, I feel her with me always.

The magic of first love
is our ignorance
that it can ever end.

—*Benjamin Disraeli*

No Man Is an Island

♡

No man is an island, entire of itself;

every man is a piece of the continent, a part of the main;

if a clod be washed away by the sea,

Europe is the less, as well as if a promontory were,

as well as if any manner of thy friends or of thine own were;

any man's death diminishes me, because I am involved in mankind.

And therefore, never send to know for whom the bell tolls;

it tolls for thee.

—JOHN DONNE

Be Loving

♡

Love Looks Up

♡

The reason why all men honor love
is because it looks up, and not down;
aspires and not despairs.

—RALPH WALDO EMERSON

Alice in Wonderland

♡

And the moral of that is—
"Oh, 'tis love, 'tis love,
that makes the world
go round!"

—LEWIS CARROLL

Peace

♡

What kind of peace do I mean?

What kind of peace do we seek?

Not a Pax Americana enforced on the world

by American weapons of war.

Not the peace of the grave or the security of the slave.

I am talking about genuine peace,

the kind of peace that makes life on earth worth living,

the kind that enables men and nations to grow

and to hope and to build a better life for their children—

not merely peace for Americans

but peace for all men and women—

not merely peace in our time but peace for all time.

—*JOHN F. KENNEDY*

911

♡

NEWSPAPER HEADLINES AND TELEVISION NEWS can sometimes
make it seem we live in a world filled with hate and violence. If only one
story dispels this myth for me, it must be about the people aboard the
planes that crashed into the World Trade Center on September 11, 2001.
None of the frantic calls that went out to friends and family were about
hate. Three words were repeated more than any others: "I Love You."

In this world, hate never dispelled hate.

Only love dispels hate.

This is the law, ancient and inexhaustible.

—BUDDHA

Love Drives Out Hate

♡

A GIRL I KNOW had tried to commit suicide multiple times. Now she touches the Open Heart symbol, which to her serves as a powerful reminder that she can survive the moments that put her in darkness and appreciate the miracle of life.

The ultimate weakness of violence is that
it is a descending spiral,
begetting the very thing it seeks to destroy . . .
Darkness cannot drive out darkness;
only light can do that.
Hate cannot drive out hate;
only love can do that.

—DR. MARTIN LUTHER KING, JR.

The Only Enemy

♡

The greatest crime is indifference and apathy to the plight of others.

—*Stacy Keach, Sr.*

The Shape of the Heart

♡

HOW IMPORTANT THIS IS, to understand that you must love but not give up your individuality, but how difficult to achieve. The linked hearts symbol suggests a measure of freedom, love which is linked but not restricted and enclosed. This is one of the personal stories sent to me about the meaning of "Open Hearts":

Just as I fell more and more in love, my mother was going through a shattering divorce which was destroying her. In this world of divorces and fractured relationships, we have still to be brave enough to love, but sensible enough to hang on to the core of who we are. I don't want ever to be destroyed by my love.

The open heart symbolizes what I want out of love. I want my heart to be

joined with another person but for both of us to maintain the core pieces of ourselves. Just as the two hearts meld into crystals in the Open Hearts jewelry, so too can two people meld to become one. But the essential shape of the heart remains. If you believe in the power of love, your relationship and individuality will both withstand the merge that occurs when two people join.

—MELISSA AMEN

Back to Work

♡

THE OVERWHELMING FEELING OF LOVE that runs through your entire being when you see your child for the first time—this is love.

. . . My darling girl

Sleeps and smiles and laughs, her face

So full of curiosity and magic

That I know the world was

Made in her honor.

She looks around her and as she looks

She renews all she sees.

The leaves rustle excitedly,

The curtains dance by the window,

The shadow moves beside her as

She turns and she turns and she turns,

Ocean eyes,

Taking it all in.

—*SALLY EMERSON*

A Mother's Power

♡

It was Mother Teresa's mother

who first encouraged her to give love to those in pain

and dying. Mother Teresa went on to show the world

about compassion and an unconditional love

that transcends religion and all boundaries.

When we see God
in each other,
we will be able to live
in peace.

—*MOTHER TERESA*

The Thousandth Man

♡

THE FRIEND to whom you can show your feelings,
and count on whatever happens, is priceless.

One man in a thousand, Solomon says,
Will stick more close than a brother.
And it's worth while seeking him half your days
If you find him before the other.
Nine hundred and ninety-nine depend
On what the world sees in you,
But the Thousandth Man will stand your friend
With the whole round world agin' you.

'Tis neither promise nor prayer nor show
Will settle the finding for 'ee.
Nine hundred and ninety-nine of 'em go
By your looks, or your acts, or your glory.

Be Loving

But if he finds you and you find him,
The rest of the world don't matter;
For the Thousandth Man will sink or swim
With you in any water.

You can use his purse with no more talk
Than he uses yours for his spendings,
And laugh and meet in your daily walk
As though there had been no lendings.
Nine hundred and ninety-nine of 'em call
For silver and gold in their dealings;
But the Thousandth Man, he's worth 'em all
Because you can show him your feelings.

His wrong's your wrong, and his right's your right,
In season or out of season.
Stand up and back it in all men's sight—
With *that* for your only reason!
Nine hundred and ninety-nine can't bide
The shame or mocking or laughter,
But the Thousandth Man will stand by your side
To the gallows-foot—and after!

—RUDYARD KIPLING

The Friendship of Helen Keller and Anne Sullivan

♡

HERE IS THE STORY of how both pupil and teacher had their lives transformed by their relationship. The person who gives gains as much as the person who learns.

Helen Keller was not yet two years old when illness stole her sight and hearing. She became, in her words, "wild and unruly, giggling and chuckling to express pleasure; kicking, scratching, uttering the choked screams of the deaf-mute to indicate the opposite." But then Anne Sullivan came to Helen's home in Alabama in March 1887, when Helen was six, from an institute for the blind in Boston. She transformed the unhappy child's life with her endless open heartedness. Helen wrote about Anne's arrival in *The Story of My Life*:

I felt approaching footsteps. I stretched out my hand as I supposed to my mother. Someone took it, and I was caught up and held close in the arms of her who had come to reveal all things to me, and, more than all things else, to love me.

Less than two weeks after that arrival Anne had written:

My heart is singing with joy this morning. A miracle has happened! The light of understanding has shone upon my little pupil's mind, and behold, all things are changed! The wild creature of two weeks ago has been transformed into a gentle child.

Love Your Neighbor

♡

He who loves his neighbor has fulfilled the law.

The commandments "You shall not commit adultery,"

"You shall not kill," "You shall not steal,"

"You shall not covet," and any other commandment

are summed up in this sentence:

"You shall love your neighbor as yourself."

Love does no wrong to a neighbor;

therefore, love is the fulfilling of the law.

—POPE BENEDICT XVI

Judaism and the Open Heart

♡

The ring in a Jewish wedding is placed on the forefinger
of the right hand. The outstretching of the right arm forms a
straight line to the heart. Symbolically, the ring is being placed
"near the heart"—the site of emotion. We say, "I love you
with all my heart." The implication goes further.
We come to know that love defines our lives in many ways.
Love exposes us, leaves us vulnerable,
and it also teaches us a great deal about ourselves.
A poet once said, "Love me, so I will know who I am."

—RABBI GERALD I. WOLPE

Acts of Kindness

♡

HERE WE SEE AGAIN how much a small gesture, like putting pen to paper or sending a card can mean. This account is from my sister.

A most wonderful and unexpected outcome of my near-fatal brain aneurysm was the deluge of cards, flowers, and messages of love and support that came flooding to me from family, friends, and acquaintances; people whose lives I unwittingly touched. I was supported on a raft of love and my complete recovery left me with an abiding belief in the kindness and openheartedness of my fellow man.

—SALLY FRANKENBERG

Friendship

♡

TO HAVE AN OPEN HEART means being open to seeing beyond what the world sees, to see instead through the "eyes of the soul." A young woman shared this story with me.

At the age of twenty-four, I learned that an infection I had fought most of my life was about to claim my leg. I was terrified of the surgery and what it would mean. But my best friend listened with her heart and knew that my fear was much more than even about losing my leg; it was the fear of any young woman—how will I look to the world?

Without my knowledge, my friend arranged for me to have my hair highlighted a few days before the operation, something I had longed to do but had not been able to afford. I cannot tell you what that small gesture of kindness meant to me. You see, it enabled me to feel "pretty" even when I got my first glimpse of my missing limb. It was my girlfriend's open heart that was able to hear what my own heart was really saying.

—*MARY ANN MARINO*

Open

♡

Painting Beauty
♡

THE OPEN HEART CAN SEE AND connect with the beauty of the world.
When I started painting, I lost myself in the world of watercolor. I couldn't
stop painting. It was an amazing therapy for me and still has the power to lift
my spirits.

Right now a moment of time is fleeting by! Capture its reality in paint!
To do that we must put all else out of our minds. We must become that
moment, make ourselves a sensitive recording plate . . . Give the image
of what we actually see, forgetting everything that has been seen before
our time.

—PAUL CÉZANNE

58

Out of Sight

♡

It is only with the heart
that one can see rightly;
what is essential
is invisible to the eye.

—ANTOINE DE SAINT-EXUPÉRY

Be Aware

♡

THIS PASSAGE IS BY A FREEDOM FIGHTER who spent eleven years as a political prisoner in Burma. It is an extraordinary account of the importance of awareness and focus. He writes, "Life is what you make it now."

As for me, don't worry. What I care about the most, and practice off and on throughout the day, is to be aware. That's all. To be awake. See, I have pieces of paper in my pockets that I carry with me: quotes, inspiring reminders. They refocus my mind on the here and now. That is the most important thing to me. To be present. Awake. Aware. My eleven years in prison were severe, but I used the time to my advantage. I never forget what I am seeing now—the pale

green line streaking across the pond, or the shadow of the tree across your

leg—disappears the moment I turn my face. This is life's simplicity. Just the here

and now. Aware that nothing is permanent. . . . Life is what you make it now.

—U Kyi Maung

Children

♡

WHOSE HEART is more "open" than that of a child?

Unless you become like little children,
you will never enter
the kingdom of heaven.

—MATTHEW (18: 3)

The Iron Lung and the Open Heart

♡

MY FRIEND DIANNE ODELL lived in an iron lung

for fifty-seven years, the result of having

contracted polio as a child.

You can only really love when you give it away.

Worn with Love

♡

HOW RARE AND HEARTBREAKING it can be to be "real,"
to really love and be loved. These words are from *The Velveteen Rabbit*,
the story of a toy who becomes greatly loved:

It doesn't happen often to people who break easily,
or have sharp edges or who have to be carefully kept.
Generally, by the time you are Real, most of your hair
has been loved off, and your eyes drop out
and you get loose in the joints and very shabby.

—MARGERY WILLIAMS

The Heart Speaks

♡

LISTENING CAN TAKE CARE OF A LOT of the murkiness in a relationship;
it's all about trying to comprehend the other person's wishes,
rather than bend their wishes to yours.

If I really listen with an open heart, I have a chance of seeing the whole of someone, on a number of levels. An open heart, like an open door, lets in light and banishes the darkness of misunderstanding. And the more light there is, the more I can see.

—BONNIE LEONG

*If I Can Stop
One Heart from Breaking*

♡

If I can stop one heart from breaking,

I shall not live in vain,

If I can ease one life the aching

Or cool one pain,

Or help one fainting robin

Unto his nest again

I shall not live in vain;

—EMILY DICKINSON

Treat People as They Ought to Be

♡

I have come to the frightening conclusion

that I am the decisive element.

It is my personal approach that creates the climate.

It is my daily mood that makes the weather.

I possess tremendous power to make

life miserable or joyous.

I can be a tool of torture or an instrument of inspiration,

I can humiliate or humor, hurt or heal.

In all situations, it is my response that decides

whether a crisis is escalated or de-escalated,

and a person is humanized or de-humanized.

If we treat people as they are, we make them worse.

If we treat people as they ought to be,

we help them become

what they are capable

of becoming.

—*GOETHE*

Romantic

♡

Romeo and Juliet

♡

JULIET: Goodnight, goodnight! as sweet repose and rest

Come to my heart as that within my breast!

ROMEO: O! wilt thou leave me so unsatisfied?

JULIET: What satisfaction canst thou have tonight?

ROMEO: The exchange of thy love's faithful vow for mine.

JULIET: I gave thee mine before thou didst request it;

And yet I would it were to give again.

ROMEO: Wouldst thou withdraw it? for what purpose, love?

JULIET: But to be frank, and give it thee again.

And yet I wish but for the thing I have

My bounty is as boundless as the sea,

My love as deep: the more I give to thee.

The more I have, for both are infinite.

—WILLIAM SHAKESPEARE

How Do I Love Thee?

♡

How do I love thee? Let me count the ways.
I love thee to the depth and breadth and height
My soul can reach, when feeling out of sight
For the ends of Being and ideal Grace.
I love thee to the level of everyday's
Most quiet need, by sun and candlelight.
I love thee freely, as men strive for Right;
I love thee purely, as they turn from Praise.
I love thee with the passion put to use
In my old griefs and with my childhood's faith.
I love thee with a love I seemed to lose
With my lost saints,—I love thee with the breath,
Smiles, tears, of all my life!—and, if God choose,
I shall but love thee better after death.

—*ELIZABETH BARRETT BROWNING*

Somewhere in Time

♡

IN 1980 I STARRED IN THE FILM *Somewhere in Time*. Richard Matheson wrote the beautiful screenplay from which this oft-quoted speech that I make to Christopher Reeve is taken:

The man of my dreams has almost faded now. The one I have created in my mind. The sort of man each woman dreams of, in the deepest and most secret reaches of her heart. I can almost see him now before me. What would I say to him if he were really here? "Forgive me. I have never known this feeling. I have lived without it all my life. Is it any wonder, then, I failed to recognize you? You, who brought it to me for the first time? Is there any way that I can tell you how my life has changed? Any way at all to let you know what sweetness you have given me? There is so much to say. I cannot find the words. Except for these: 'I love you.'" Such would I say to him if he were really here.

No Less, But More

♡

These two are not two
Love has made them one
Amo, Amo Ergo Sum!
And by its mystery
Each is no less but more.

—"A WEDDING ANTHEM"

No Choice

♡

"Fools rush in where angels fear to tread."

I think love is so important

that it doesn't matter that it's vulnerable.

When you fall in love,

you feel you have no choice, but in a sense,

it's the freest thing you ever do.

—CICELY SAUNDERS

To My Dear and Loving Husband

♡

If ever two were one, then surely we,
    If ever man were lov'd by wife, then thee;
If ever wife was happy in a man,
    Compare with me ye women, if you can.
I prize thy love more than whole Mines of gold,
    Or all the riches that the East doth hold.

My love is such that Rivers cannot quench,
    Nor ought but love from thee, give recompense.
Thy love is such I can no way repay,
    The heavens reward thee manifold, I pray.
Then while we live, in love let's so persevere,
    That when we have no more, we may live ever.

—Ann Bradstreet

The Dance of Love

♡

THIS PERFECTLY EXPRESSES the open heart image; the idea of a couple as dancers, neither possessing the other, but being equal partners in a complex series of moves.

When you love someone, you do not love them all the time, in exactly the same way, from moment to moment. It is an impossibility. It is even a lie to pretend to. And yet this is exactly what most of us demand. We have so little faith in the ebb and flow of life, of love, of relationships. We leap at the flow of the tide and resist in terror its ebb. We are afraid it will never return. We insist on permanency, on duration, on continuity; when the only continuity possible, in life as in love, is in growth, in fluidity—in freedom, in the sense that the dancers are free, barely touching as they pass, but partners in the same pattern.

—ANNE MORROW LINDBERGH

"Love"

Jane Seymour

Love is My Religion

♡

I cannot exist without you—I am forgetful of every thing but seeing you again—my life seems to stop there—I see no further. You have absorbed me.

I have a sensation at the present moment as though I were dissolving . . . I have been astonished that men could die martyrs for religion—I have shuddered at it—I shudder no more—I could be martyred for my religion—love is my religion—I could die for that—I could die for you. My creed is love and you are its only tenet—you have ravished me away by a power I cannot resist.

—*JOHN KEATS TO FANNY BRAWNE, 1819*

Brave
♡

Wounded by Understanding

♡

Love has no other desire but to fulfill itself.

But if you love and must needs have desires, let

these be your desires:

To melt and be like a running brook that sings its

melody to the night.

To know the pain of too much tenderness.

To be wounded by your own understanding of love;

And to bleed willingly and joyfully.

To wake at dawn with a winged heart and to give

thanks for another day of loving;

To rest at the noon hour and meditate love's ecstasy;

To return home at eventide with gratitude;

And then to sleep with a prayer for the beloved in

your heart and a song of praise upon your lips.

—*Kahlil Gibran*

An Unbreakable Heart

♡

To love at all is to be vulnerable. Love anything, and your heart will certainly be wrung and possibly be broken. If you want to make sure of keeping it intact, you must give your heart to no one, not even to an animal. Wrap it carefully round with hobbies and little luxuries; avoid all entanglements; lock it up safe in the casket or coffin of your selfishness. But in that casket—safe, dark, motionless, airless—it will change. It will not be broken; it will become unbreakable, impenetrable, irredeemable.

—C. S. Lewis

Wrong

♡

I ENCOUNTERED A WOMAN who lost her daughter, an aspiring dancer,
in a tragic drunk-driving accident. She processed her grief by doing something
in her daughter's memory. She now runs a charity that helps others through
dance therapy. Her open heart helped her heal and gave her purpose,
a chance to help people.

It is wrong to sorrow without ceasing.

—HOMER

On Pain

♡

GRIEF AND BEING HURT is a part of living.

This passage from *The Prophet* is saying that all life is a miracle and a wonder,

and sadness is as much a part of that wonder as joy. It is life.

Your pain is the breaking of the shell that encloses your understanding.

Even as the stone of the fruit must break,

that its heart may stand in the sun, so must you know pain.

And could you keep your heart in wonder at the daily miracles of your life,

your pain would not seem less wondrous than your joy;

And you would accept the seasons of your heart, even as you have always

accepted the seasons that pass over your fields.

And you would watch with serenity through the winters of your grief.

—KAHLIL GIBRAN

Create a Life of Love

♡

HERE ARE ACCOUNTS of staying strong with an open heart from a friend:

There are those times when you can actually feel your heart break from personal pain . . . I sat in a small room crying after hearing my son was sentenced to seven years in prison. Had I not believed that my open heart would one day heal me, I fear I would have died from the mental pain.

My daughter was aged fifteen when she insisted on living with her dad and not me. I never gave up calling her and leaving messages, sending cards with lots of love. I kept hope for what seemed like a miracle—that one day she would want to be with me again. Today she's twenty and we are inseparable.

—ANONYMOUS

Love Like You've Never Been Hurt

♡

THIS REMINDS US NEVER TO BE BITTER. An open heart doesn't harden and become closed because of pain. It was a great realization when I understood that you have to be brave enough to face suffering to know the depths of happiness.

As we grow up, we learn that even the one person that wasn't supposed ever to let you down probably will. You will have your heart broken probably more than once and it's harder every time. You'll break hearts too, so remember how it felt when yours was broken.

You'll fight with your best friend. You'll blame a new love for things an old one did. You'll cry because time is passing too fast, and you'll eventually lose someone you love. So take too many pictures, laugh too much, and love like you've never been hurt . . . Don't be afraid that your life will end, be afraid that it will never begin.

—*ANONYMOUS*

Gentle ♡

Give Yourself a Hug

♡

Give yourself a hug
when you feel unloved

Give yourself a hug
when people put on airs
to make you feel a bug

Give yourself a hug
when everyone seems to give you
a cold-shoulder shrug

Give yourself a hug—
a big, big hug

And keep on singing,
"Only one in a million like me
Only one in a million-billlion-
trillion-zillion
like me."

—GRACE NICHOLS

Divine You

♡

Hold up your hands
before your eyes.
You are looking
at the hands of God.

—RABBI LAWRENCE KUSHNER

Open to Everything

♡

THOSE WHO ARE CURIOUS ABOUT EVERYTHING in the world, open to everything, have rich lives. The writer points out that we should be curious, too, about ourselves.

One road to happiness is to cultivate curiosity about everything. Not only about people but about subjects, not only about the arts but about history and foreign customs. Not only about countries and cities but about plants and animals. Not only about lichened rocks and curious markings on the bark of trees, but about stars and atoms. Not only about our friends but about that strange labyrinth we inhabit which we call ourselves. Then, if we do that, we will never suffer a moment's boredom.

—*GERALD BRENAN*

Do It Now

♡

I expect to pass through life but once.
If, therefore, there be any kindness
I can show, or any good thing I can do
to any fellow being, let me do it now,
for I shall not pass this way again.

—WILLIAM PENN

The Sin of Omission

♡

It isn't the thing you do, dear,
  It's the thing you leave undone
That gives you a bit of a heartache
  At setting of the sun.
The tender word forgotten,
  The letter you did not write,
The flowers you did not send, dear,
  Are your haunting ghosts at night.

The stone you might have lifted
  Out of a brother's way;
The bit of heartsome counsel
  You were hurried too much to say;
The loving touch of the hand, dear,
  The gentle, winning tone
Which you had no time nor thought for
  With troubles enough of your own.

Gentle

Those little acts of kindness
    So easily out of mind,
Those chances to be angels
    Which we poor mortals find—
They come in night and silence,
    Each sad, reproachful wraith,
When hope is faint and flagging,
    And a chill has fallen on faith.

For life is all too short, dear,
    And sorrow is all too great,
To suffer our slow compassion
    That tarries until too late;
And it isn't the thing you do, dear,
    It's the thing you leave undone
Which gives you a bit of heartache
    At the setting of the sun.

—Margaret E. Sangster

The Good

♡

THIS POEM TELLS OF THE VULNERABLE GRACE of the good. We don't respect the good enough in our culture, where winners take all.

The good are vulnerable

As any bird in flight,

They do not think of safety,

Are blind to possible extinction

And when most vulnerable

Are most themselves.

The good are as real as the sun,

Are best perceived through clouds

Of casual corruption

Gentle

That cannot kill the
luminous sufficiency

That shines on city, sea,
and wilderness,

Fastidiously revealing

One man to another,

Who yet will not accept

Responsibilities of light.

The good incline to praise,

To have the knack of seeing that

The best is not destroyed

Although forever threatened.

The good go naked
in all weathers,

And by their nakedness rebuke

The small protective sanities

That hide men from themselves.

The good are difficult to see

Though open, rare, destructible;

Always, they retain a kind of youth,

The vulnerable grace

Of any bird in flight,

Content to be itself,

Accomplished master and
potential victim,

Accepting what the earth
or sky intends.

I think that I know one or two

Among my friends.

—BRENDAN KENNELLY

Open to Nature

♡

Androcles and the Lion

♡

THE OPEN HEART GIVES BECAUSE IT WISHES TO, expecting nothing in return. But often, directly or indirectly, there is a return, even if it is simply feeling better because you have helped to create a kinder, more benevolent atmosphere around yourself. Or the recipient of your kindness may be kind to someone else. Or your kindness is repaid in a way you could not expect.

There once was a poor slave whose name was Androcles. His master mistreated him and Androcles ran away into the forest, where a lion came roaring towards him. Androcles was terrified, but then he noticed that the beast was limping, and that the frightening roar held a note of melancholy suffering. He calmly approached the animal and took the lion's paw in his hand. It was embedded with a huge thorn and very red and swollen. "Poor thing," Androcles said. He pulled gingerly at the thorn. The lion, with an angry roar of pain, jerked back his paw so abruptly that Androcles was thrown on his back. "Sorry," said Androcles. He gave the thorn another pull. The lion roared and snapped his jaws, but Androcles persevered. One more pull and the thorn came out. The lion shook his paw wildly. "That's it," said Androcles, holding up the thorn.

Time passed. Androcles was recaptured and sent to be eaten by the wild beasts in the arena. One was a lion, who roared and leapt towards him. Androcles was preparing for his death when he felt the lick of the animal's tongue and looked up to see his old friend, the lion, whose thorn he had extracted. He flung his arms around him. There was a moment of silent shock from the crowd, then a murmur and finally, a cheer.

Pied Beauty

♡

THIS POEM IS IN PRAISE OF THE BEAUTY all around us.
This appreciation for nature and our surroundings is something those
with an open heart, regardless of creed, can share.

Glory be to God for dappled things—

    For skies of couple-color as a brinded cow;

        For rose-moles all in stipple upon trout that swim;

Fresh-firecoal chestnut-falls; finches' wings;

    Landscape plotted and pieced—fold, fallow, and plough;

        And all trades, their gear and tackle and trim.

All things counter, original, spare, strange;

Whatever is fickle, freckled (who knows how?)

With swift, slow; sweet, sour; adazzle, dim;

He fathers-forth whose beauty is past change:

Praise him.

—*GERARD MANLEY HOPKINS*

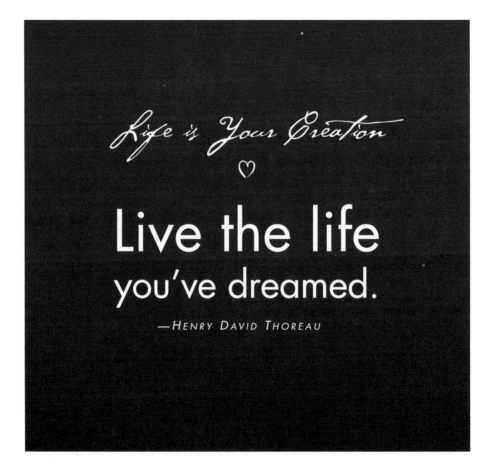

Life is Your Creation

♡

Live the life
you've dreamed.

—HENRY DAVID THOREAU

Where the Bee Sucks, There Suck I

♡

Where the bee sucks, there suck I;

In a cowslip's bell I lie;

There I couch when owls do cry,

On the bat's back I do fly

After summer merrily,

Merrily, merrily shall I live now

Under the blossom that hangs on the bough.

—WILLIAM SHAKESPEARE

Open to Challenges

♡

The Way to Love

♡

. . . If I have the gift of prophecy and fathom all mysteries and all knowledge, and if I have all faith that can move mountains, but have not love, I am nothing. If I give all I possess to the poor and surrender my body to the flames, but have not love, I gain nothing.

Love is patient, love is kind. It does not envy, it does not boast, it is not proud. It is not rude, it is not self-seeking, it is not easily angered, it keeps no record of wrongs. Love does not delight in evil but rejoices with the truth. It always protects, always trusts, always hopes, always perseveres.

Love never fails. But where there are prophecies, they will cease; where there are tongues, they will be stilled; where there is knowledge, it will pass away. For we know in part and we prophesy in part, but when perfection comes, the imperfect disappears. When I was a child, I talked like a child, I thought like a child, I reasoned like a child. When I became a man, I put childish ways behind me. Now we see but a poor reflection as in a mirror; then we shall see face to face. Now I know in part; then I shall know fully, even as I am fully known.

And now these three remain: faith, hope, and love. But the greatest of these is love.

—*1 CORINTHIANS 13*

119

On Love

♡

Love is a mighty power,

a great and complete good.

Love alone lightens every burden, and makes rough places smooth.

It bears every hardship as though it were nothing, and renders all

bitterness sweet and acceptable.

Nothing is sweeter than love.

Nothing stronger.

Nothing higher.

Nothing wider.

Nothing more pleasant.

Nothing fuller or better in heaven and earth;

For love is born of God.

Love flies, runs, and leaps for joy.

It is free and unrestrained.

Love knows no limits, but ardently transcends all bounds.

Love feels no burden, takes no account of toil,

attempts things beyond its strength.

Love sees nothing as impossible,

for it feels able to achieve all things.

It is strange and effective,

while those who lack love faint and fail.

Love is not fickle and sentimental,

nor is it intent on vanities.

Like a living flame and a burning torch,

it surges upward and surely surmounts every obstacle.

—*THOMAS À KEMPIS*

The Happy Life

♡

As Coleridge said,
"We receive but what we give."
The happy life is a life
of continual generosity in which
we go out to meet and
acclaim the world.

—GERALD BRENAN

She is Gone

♡

You can shed tears that she is gone,
    or you can smile because she has lived.

Your heart can be empty because you can't see her,
    or you can be full of the love you shared.

You can turn your back on tomorrow and live yesterday,
    or you can be happy for tomorrow because of yesterday.

You can remember her and only that she's gone,
    or you can cherish her memory and let it live on.

You can cry and close your mind, be empty, and turn your back,
    or you can do what she'd want: smile, open your eyes,
    love and go on.

—ANONYMOUS

For Katrina's Sun Dial

♡

This poem was read at Princess Diana's funeral.

Time is too slow for those who wait,
Too swift for those who fear,
Too long for those who grieve,
Too short for those who rejoice,
But for those who love,
time is Eternity.

—HENRY VAN DYKE

New Every Morning

♡

Every day is a fresh beginning,

Listen my soul to the glad refrain.

And, spite of old sorrows

And older sinning,

Troubles forecasted

And possible pain,

Take heart with the day and begin again.

—*SUSAN COOLIDGE*

ART TITLES AND DESCRIPTIONS

Page 2: Open Heart: Watercolor on paper, 5 x 7"

Page 5: Healing Hearts: Heart for Fletcher: Watercolor on paper, 7 x 5"

Page 6: Open Hearts: Peace, Love, and an Open Heart: Mixed media on paper, 10 ½ x 8 ¼"

Page 7: Heart III: Watercolor on paper, 5 ⅛ x 5 ⅛"

Page 12: Healing Hearts: Red, Blue, & Yellow: Acrylic on canvas, 12 x 12"

Page 15: Healing Hearts in the Open Field: Acrylic on canvas, 8 x 10"

Page 16: Portrait of a Shasta Daisy: Oil on canvas, 24 x 24"

Page 23: Healing Hearts: Hearts Together Yellow & Red: Watercolor on paper, 6 x 9"

Page 24: Open Heart: Watercolor on paper, 5 x 7"

Page 27: Heart III: Watercolor on paper, 5 ⅛ x 5 ⅛"

Page 29: Red Tulips in a Clear Vase: Oil on board, 18 x 14"

Page 30: Healing Hearts: Hearts on Fire Blue & Yellow: Acrylic on paper, 12 x 12"

Page 35: Healing Hearts: Red & Yellow: Watercolor on paper, 5 ⅝ x 4 ⅞"

Page 37: Dreams of Giverny: Oil on canvas, 48 x 36"

Page 41: Healing Hearts: Love Entwined VI Red & Yellow: Watercolor on paper, 6 ¼ x 9"

Page 43: Heart IV: Watercolor on paper, 5 ½ x 4 ½"

Page 45: Heart III: Watercolor on paper, 5 ⅛ x 5 ⅛"

Page 49: Open Heart: Watercolor on paper, 5 x 7"

Page 50: Healing Hearts: Family of Hearts Magenta & Yellow: Watercolor on paper, 8 ½ x 11"

Page 55: Healing Hearts: Hearts Together Yellow & Red: Watercolor on paper, 6 x 9"

Page 56: Valentine's Day Bouquet: Watercolor on paper with pen and ink, 7 x 5"

Page 61: Heart IV: Watercolor on paper, 5 ½ x 4 ½"

Page 63: Women Growing Together II: Watercolor on paper, 24 x 18"

Page 67: Healing Hearts: Heart for Fletcher: Watercolor on paper, 7 x 5"

For further information on The Art of Jane Seymour, please contact Coral Canyon Publishing at www.janeseymour.com.

Acknowledgments

Sally Emerson, Susan Nagy Luks, Cheri Ingle, Debra Pearl, Susan Ginsburg, and all those I've met in the galleries and on the internet who continue to inspire me with their open heart stories and JB Robinson, Belden, Marks & Morgan, Shaw's,

Osterman, Goodman, LeRoy's, Weisfield, Rogers, Friedlander's, Kay Jewelers, and Jared the Galleria of Jewelry, at Running Press: Jon Anderson, Bill Jones, and Cindy De La Hoz.

In loving memory of those who are no longer with us—Sydney Schlobohm, Fletcher Vines, and Dianne Odell. Their open heart stories will live on through the people whose lives they have touched.

─────────

BIBLIOGRAPHY

Page 14: Tolle, Eckhart. *A New Earth*. New York: Dutton, 2005.

Page 19: Walsch, Neale Donald. *Friendship with God: An Uncommon Dialogue*. New York: Berkley, 2002.

Page 42: Emerson, Sally. *Occasional Poets*. New York: Viking, 1986. Reprinted by permission of Curtis Brown Group, UK.

Page 51: Ratzinger, Joseph. *Catechism of the Catholic Church*. Washington, D.C., USCCB, 2005.

Pages 60–61: Clements, Alan. *Instinct for Freedom*. Novato, CA: New World Library, 2006.

Page 76: Passage from *Somewhere in Time* reprinted by permission of Don Congdon Associates, Inc. © 1980 by Richard Matheson.

Page 79: © copyright 1949 by Boosey & Co. Limited

Page 82: From *Gift from the Sea* by Anne Morrow Lindbergh, © copyright 1955, 1975, renewed 1983 by Anne Morrow Lindbergh. Used by permission of Pantheon Books.

Pages 88–89, 92: Gibran, Kahlil. *The Prophet*. First published in 1923.

Page 90: *The Four Loves* by C.S. Lewis copyright © c.s. Lewis Pte. Ltf. 1960. Used by permission of Houghton Mifflin Harcourt Publishing Company.

Page 98: Nichols, Grace. *Give Yourself a Hug*. United Kingdom: A & C Black, 1994.

Page 107: Kennelly, Brendan. *Familiar Strangers: New and Selected Poems 1960–2004*. United Kingdom: Bloodaxe Books, 2004.